ASTOUNDING ACTIVITIES FOR
MINECRAFTERS

Puzzles and Games for Endless Fun!

Sky Pony Press
New York

Copyright © 2019 by Hollan Publishing, Inc.

Minecraft® is a registered trademark of Notch Development AB.

The Minecraft game is copyright © Mojang AB.

Sky Pony Press books may be purchased in bulk at special discounts for sales promotion, corporate gifts, fund-raising, or educational purposes. Special editions can also be created to specifications. For details, contact the Special Sales Department, Sky Pony Press, 307 West 36th Street, 11th Floor, New York, NY 10018 or info@skyhorsepublishing.com.

Sky Pony® is a registered trademark of Skyhorse Publishing, Inc.®, a Delaware corporation.

Minecraft® is a registered trademark of Notch Development AB.
The Minecraft game is copyright © Mojang AB.

Visit our website at www.skyponypress.com.

10 9 8 7 6 5 4

Library of Congress Cataloging-in-Publication Data is available on file.

Puzzles created by Jen Funk Weber

Cover design by Brian Peterson
Cover illustration by Bill Greenhead
Interior illustrations by Amanda Brack

Print ISBN: 978-1-5107-4102-7

Printed in China

CONTENTS

WHEEL OF FORTUNE #1

Start at the ▼.
Write every third letter on the spaces to reveal a fortune you want to claim.

K E T F E E O N D R C P T H I U A C N N

F _ _ _ _ _ _ - _ _ _ _ _ _ _ _ _

_ _ _ _

5

ALEX SAYS: TOOL TIP

If you have ever played the game Simon Says, then you know how this game works: follow only the directions that begin with "Alex says" to reveal a helpful tool tip.

	1	2	3	4	5
A	IF	THE	DON'T	TO	YOU
B	WASTE	MINED	EMERALD	IRON	DIAMONDS
C	CAN'T	ON	GRIND	ISN'T	BE
D	A	KIND	REDSTONE	SHOVEL	BLIND

1. **Alex says**, "Cross off words with fewer than four letters in Row A and Column 5."

2. **Alex says**, "Cross off words that rhyme with *find*."

3. Cross off all Minecraft tools.

4. **Alex says**, "Cross off the ores in columns 3 and 4."

5. **Alex says**, "Cross off contractions in Row C."

6. **Alex says**, "Read the remaining words to reveal a tip from Alex."

Secret tip: _____

_____

THE MIRROR'S MESSAGE

Circle letters on the top half of the grid that have correct mirror images on the bottom half. Write the circled letters in order on the spaces to uncover a ghastly detail you may not know.

T H U O W O R A K S P L E A M S H P O T

I O N S M U P S T H M I T T H I A E L O

W E B R H A L O C F O F A R G O H A S T

———————————————————

W E D R H A T O D L O A P C C H A S T

I O M J S W N R S T H S I T L H W E L O

T K M O M O R A K S P J S A W S H P O T

_ _   _ _ _ _ ,   _ _ _ _ _

_ _ _ _ _ _ _ _ _   _ _ _ _ _ _   _ _ _   _ _ _

_ _ _ _ _ _ _ _ _ _ _

YOU CAN DRAW IT: WITHER

Use the grid to copy the picture. Examine each small square in the top grid, then transfer those lines to the corresponding square on the bottom grid.

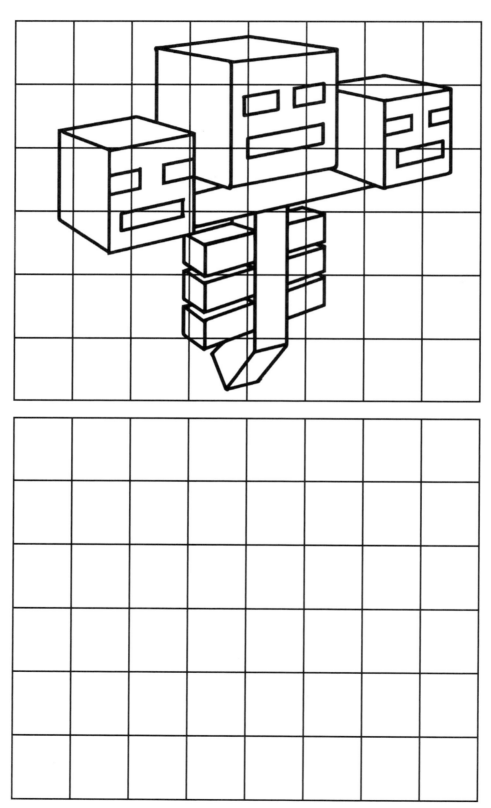

SHOP AROUND THE BLOCK

Minecraft player, Ew N. Ick, built a specialty shop that sells poisonous potato, rotten flesh, spider eye, and pufferfish. What is the name of this shop? Follow the directions in the flow chart to find out.

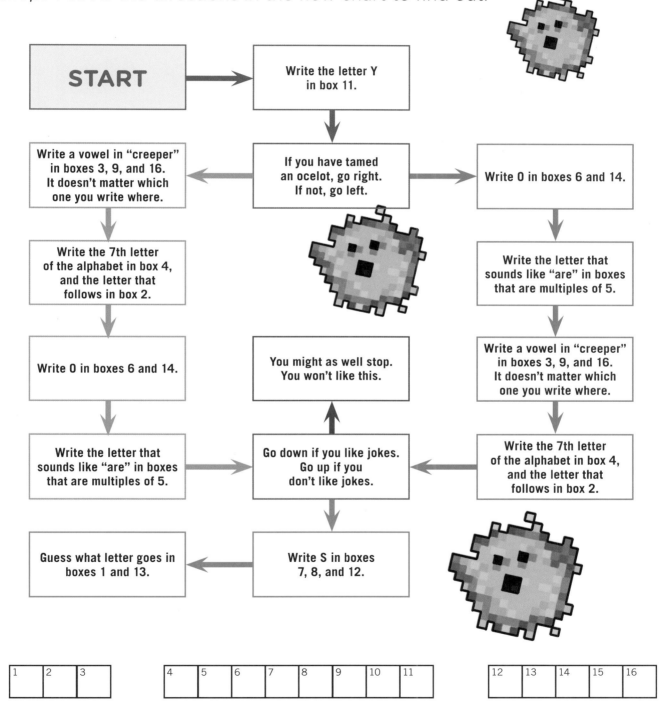

START

Write the letter Y in box 11.

If you have tamed an ocelot, go right. If not, go left.

Write a vowel in "creeper" in boxes 3, 9, and 16. It doesn't matter which one you write where.

Write O in boxes 6 and 14.

Write the 7th letter of the alphabet in box 4, and the letter that follows in box 2.

Write the letter that sounds like "are" in boxes that are multiples of 5.

Write O in boxes 6 and 14.

You might as well stop. You won't like this.

Write a vowel in "creeper" in boxes 3, 9, and 16. It doesn't matter which one you write where.

Write the letter that sounds like "are" in boxes that are multiples of 5.

Go down if you like jokes. Go up if you don't like jokes.

Write the 7th letter of the alphabet in box 4, and the letter that follows in box 2.

Guess what letter goes in boxes 1 and 13.

Write S in boxes 7, 8, and 12.

1	2	3

4	5	6	7	8	9	10	11

12	13	14	15	16

STAY AWAY!

The answers to the clues use each letter in the letter box. Write the answers to the clues on the numbered spaces, one letter on each blank. Then transfer the letters to the boxes with the same numbers. If you fill in the boxes correctly, you'll reveal something you should avoid if you're worried about zombie pigmen.

A E E H L N O P R R T T

Not now, but soon

___ ___ ___ ___ ___
1 2 3 4 5

Often a dog or cat, but sometimes a horse or snake

___ ___ ___
6 7 8

You can honk this on a car

___ ___ ___ ___
9 10 11 12

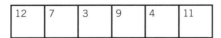

12	7	3	9	4	11

6	10	5	8	2	1

ENCHANTED CHEST

This End City chest is enchanted. To open it, you must press all nine buttons just once, in the correct order.

Follow the directions on the buttons. For instance, 2D means you must move your finger two buttons down. R=right, L=left, U=up. To open the chest, you must land on the F button last.

Which button do you have to press first to land on the F button last?

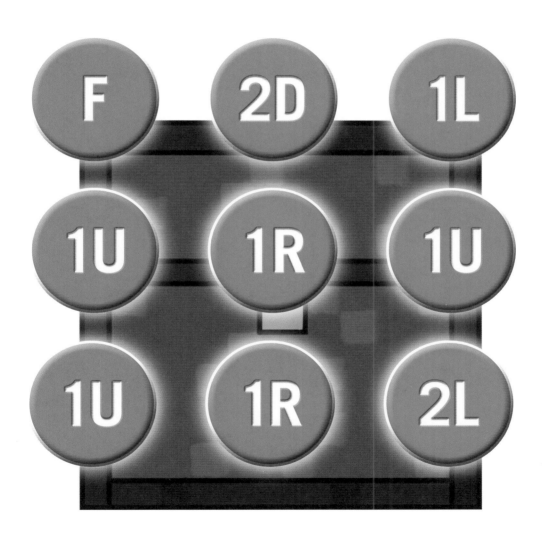

KILLER JOKE

In this crossword, you get to figure out where each word fits. Use the picture clues to guess the word answers, then see where each word fits best. If you fill in the puzzle correctly, you'll get a funny answer to the question below.

What's the difference between a killer rabbit and a counterfeit dollar bill?

 $\overline{9}$ $\overline{4}$ $\overline{13}$ $\overline{3}$ $\overline{10}$ $\overline{14}$ $\overline{5}$ $\overline{8}$ $\overline{1}$ $\overline{9}$ $\overline{4}$ $\overline{13}$ $\overline{12}$ $\overline{5}$ $\overline{4}$ $\overline{8}$

 $\overline{6}$ $\overline{11}$ $\overline{13}$ $\overline{9}$ $\overline{6}$ $\overline{11}$ $\overline{13}$ $\overline{2}$ $\overline{3}$ $\overline{10}$ $\overline{5}$ $\overline{1}$ $\overline{5}$ $\overline{8}$

 $\overline{14}$ $\overline{7}$ $\overline{4}$ $\overline{4}$ $\overline{12}$

GEM SEARCH

Can you find the emerald? It appears only once in a horizontal, vertical, or diagonal line.

```
L A E D L E R E M E
E R A M E M A M D R
D M L D E E E L E A
A L E D L R A D M D
E L A R E M E E L D
M A D R A A D A E L
E L R D M L R E D A
R M D A R E L A L R
A E A L M A E D E E
D E M E R E D L A M
```

BURIED TREASURE

Uncover the loot in the grid, and it is yours! Color every box that has an odd number to discover the name of the loot item.

13	27	9	78	77	4	92	29	50	55	3	61
44	35	10	70	83	1	18	15	16	28	97	14
26	41	62	56	21	66	49	7	38	60	19	32
12	19	8	74	5	30	2	63	54	32	43	6

YOU CAN DRAW IT: OCELOT

Use the grid to copy the picture. Examine each small square in the top grid, then transfer those lines to the corresponding square on the bottom grid.

FAVORITE THING TO DO

Follow each player's path, under and over crossing paths, to discover what each likes to do in Minecraft.

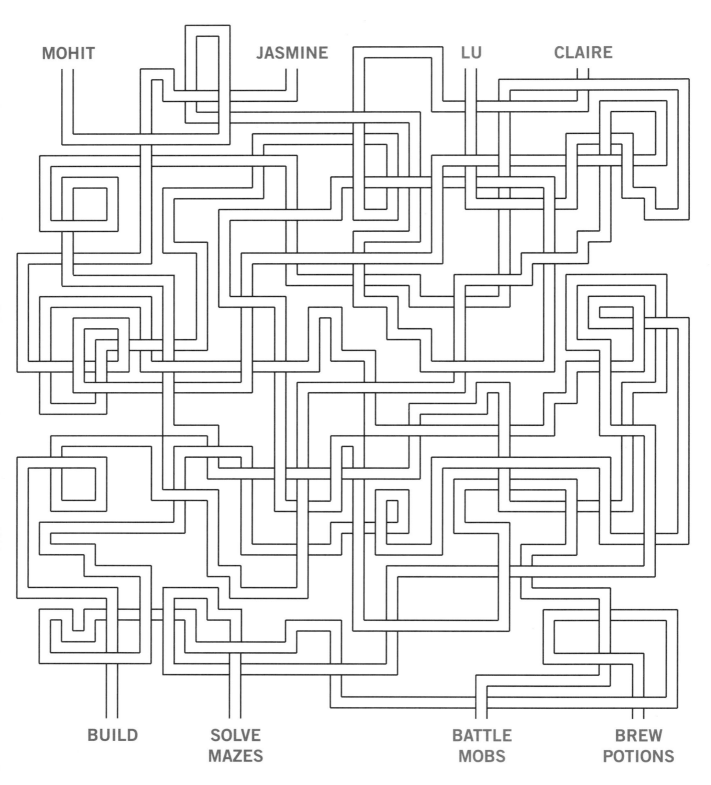

MOHIT   JASMINE   LU   CLAIRE

BUILD   SOLVE   BATTLE   BREW
               MAZES   MOBS   POTIONS

SQUARED UP: GARDEN PLOT

Each of the four vegetables in this puzzle can appear only once in each row, column, and the four inside boxes. Can you figure out how this garden plot is designed?

        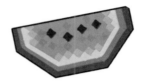

B = BEETROOT   C = CARROT   M = MELON   P = POTATO

			B
C	B		M
P		B	C
B			

HOMEWARD BOUND

Help the villager find his way back home.

START
↓

STOP

LIFE-SAVING STEPS

Boxes connected by lines contain the same letter. Some letters are given; others have to be guessed. Fill in all the boxes to reveal the answer to this question:

What steps should you take if you meet a hostile mob while you are unarmed?

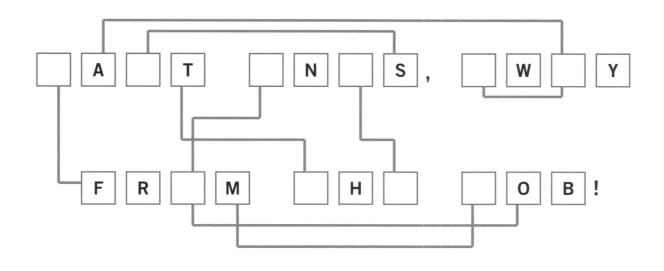

[ ] A T [ ] N S , [ ] W [ ] Y

F R [ ] M [ ] H [ ] [ ] O B !

YOU CAN DRAW IT: LLAMA

Use the grid to copy the picture. Examine one small square in the top picture then transfer those lines to the corresponding square in the bottom grid.

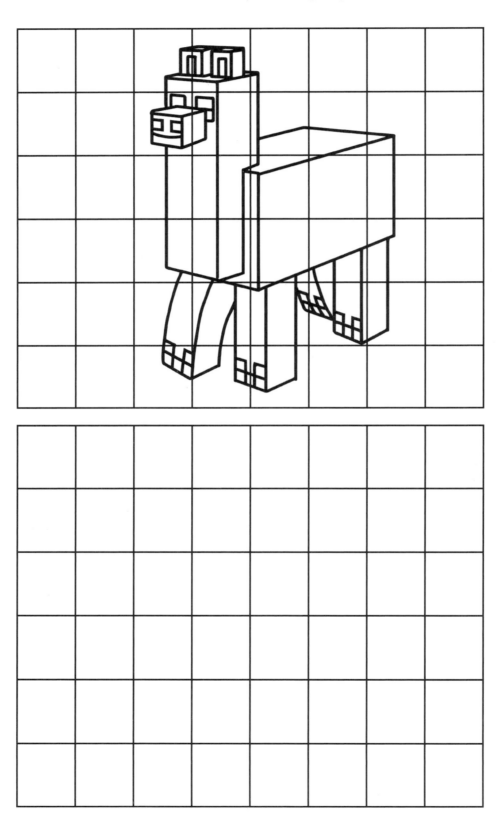

FACT OF (REAL) LIFE

The answer to the question will be revealed as you add letters to the empty boxes that come before, between, or after the given letters in the alphabet. If you get to Z, start all over again with A. The first letter has been written for you.

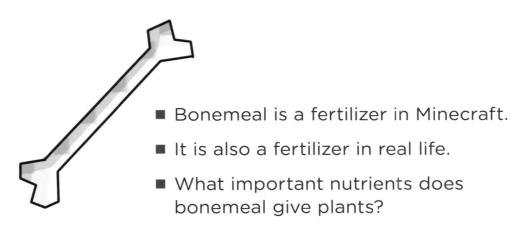

- Bonemeal is a fertilizer in Minecraft.
- It is also a fertilizer in real life.
- What important nutrients does bonemeal give plants?

| P | | | | | | | | | |

Q I P T Q I P S V T
R J Q U R J Q T W U

Z M C

| | | |

B O E

A Y J A G S K
B Z K B H T L

| | | | | | | |

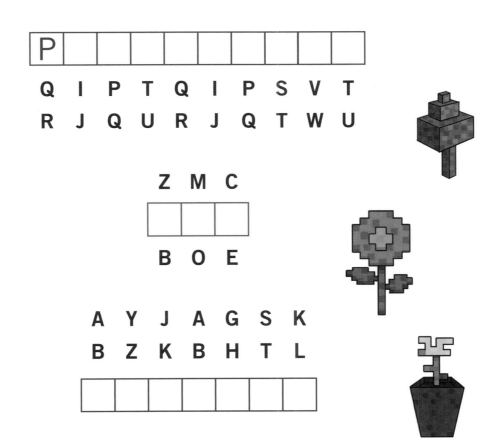

MYSTERY MOB

One mob on this page is real. The others are holograms. You must identify the one real mob from the clues below and circle it.

My first letter is in **PIGMAN**, but not in **ZOMBIE**

My second is in **FISH** and also in **WITHER**

My third is in **PARROT**, but not in **SPIDER**

My fourth is in **SHEEP**, but not **POLAR BEAR**

The fifth and fourth are next-door neighbors in the alphabet

NETHER FINDS

Find and circle names of ten things you can only collect or build if you visit The Nether. They might be forward, backward, up, down, or diagonal. Watch out! Every N has gone up in flames.

BLAZE ROD
GHAST TEARS
GLOWSTONE

MAGMA CREAM
NETHER BRICK

NETHER BRICK FENCE
NETHER BRICK STAIRS

NETHER RACK
NETHER WART
SOUL SAND

WHO'S WHOSE ON THE FARM?

Use the clues to figure out which animal belongs to which player.

- ■ BlockBuster's animal is facing left.
- ■ Creeper Hunter's animal is dyed.
- ■ iBuild's animal is not pink.
- ■ Masterminer's animal carries a chest.

	CHICKEN	DONKEY	SHEEP	PIG
BlockBuster				
iBuild				
Creeper Hunter				
Masterminer				

PARTY SNACK PICK-UP

You are picking up snacks for a party. You need to collect four pumpkin pies, four cookies, and four melon slices.

You must pick up your first snack in the top row and your last snack in the bottom row, and you must pick them up in this order:

Moving only up, down, left, and right, what path must you take?

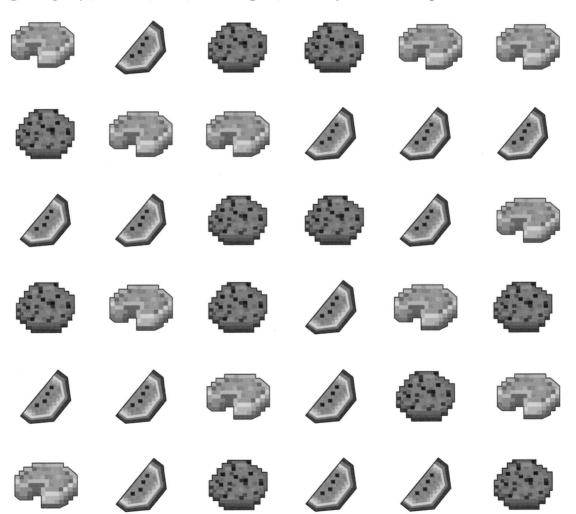

GET OUT!

Can you find your way out of this maze alive?

START

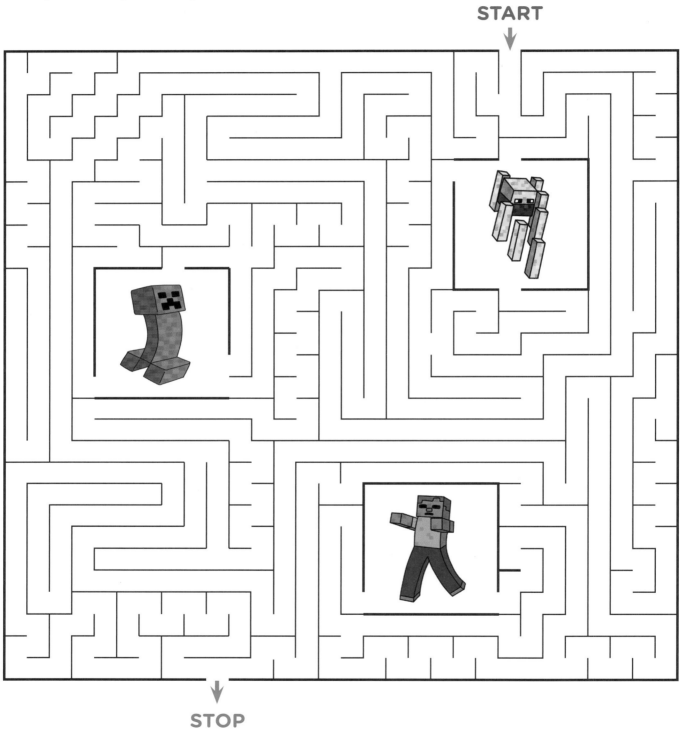

STOP

YOU CAN DRAW IT: SKELETON

Use the grid to copy the picture. Examine each small square in the top grid, then transfer those lines to the corresponding square on the bottom grid.

WISHING YOU GOOD . . .

Every word in Column B contains the same letters as a word in Column A, plus one letter. Draw a line between word "matches," then write the extra letter on the space provided. Unscramble the column of letters to reveal our wish for your Minecraft avatar—and for you, too. And your family. And friends. And pets. Well, you get the idea.

COLUMN A	COLUMN B	EXTRA LETTER
Term	Ocean	__
Dared	Heart	__
Rate	Crash	__
Once	Death	__
Scar	Meter	__
Head	Ladder	__

__ __ __ __ __

RARE DROP SCORES

Four Minecraft players scored rare drops today. Who collected what?

To find out, begin at the dot below each player's name and follow it downward. Every time you hit a horizontal line (one that goes across), you must take it. See where each player's path leads.

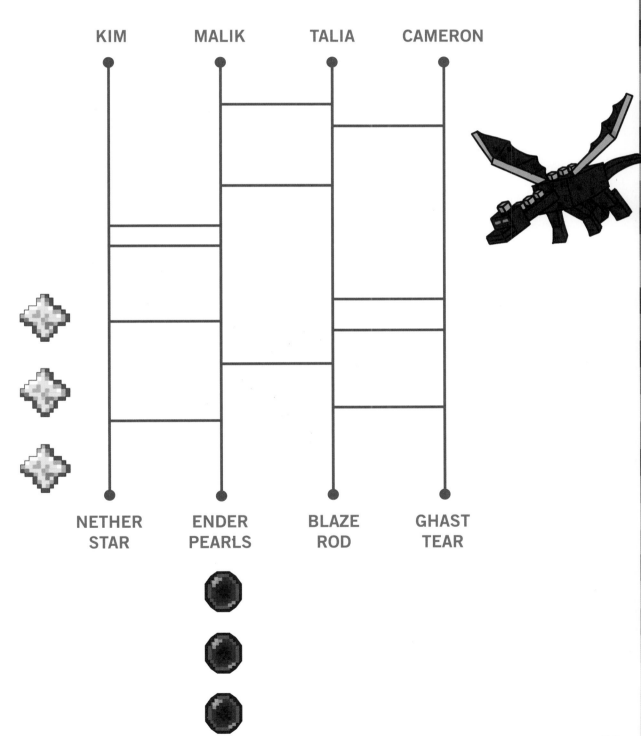

KIM   MALIK   TALIA   CAMERON

NETHER   ENDER   BLAZE   GHAST
STAR   PEARLS   ROD   TEAR

LOST LIBRARY

Four players are racing to find a book of maps in the library in a woodland mansion. Follow each player's path, under and over crossing paths, to discover who finds the book that will save them all.

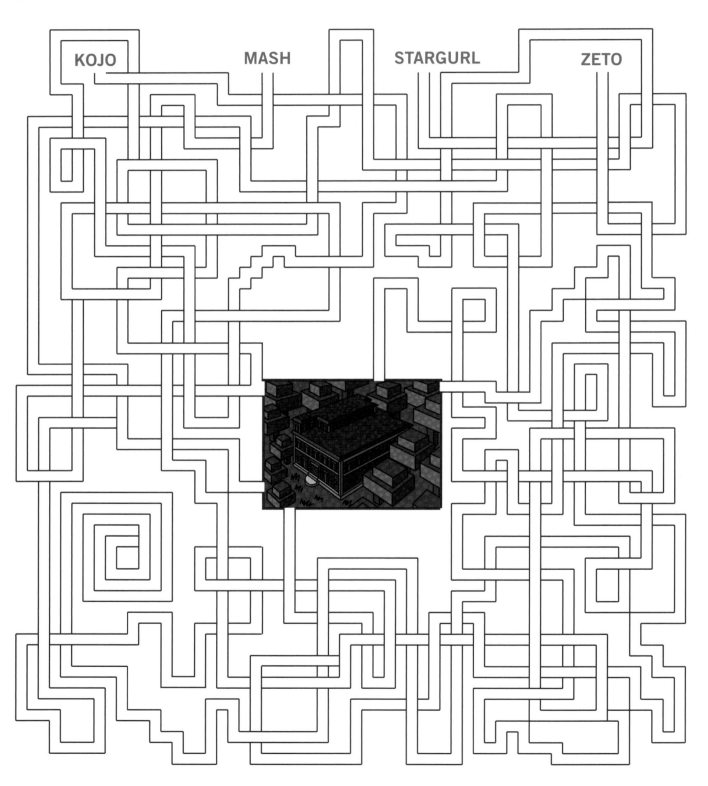

KOJO MASH STARGURL ZETO

UNCOMMON COMMON FEATURE

In this crossword, you get to figure out where each word fits! Use the picture clues to guess the word answers, then see where each word fits best. If you fill in the puzzle correctly, you'll discover something uncommon that a few villagers have in common. Got that?

D I A M O N D S W O R D

F L I N T

What do a librarian, priest, and nitwit have in common?

___ ___ ___ ___ ___ ___   ___ ___ ___ ___ ___   ___ ___
7   4   7   6   10 2   11 9   9   2   6   9   4

___ ___ ___ ___ ___   ___ ___ ___ ___ ___
1   11 10 3   8   8   9   5   10 6

ALEX SAYS: DID YOU KNOW THIS ABOUT ZOMBIES?

If you have ever played the game Simon Says, then you know how this game works: follow only the directions that begin with "Alex says" to reveal a tip about zombies.

	1	2	3	4	5
A	WHO	IF	HOW	ZOMBIES	THROW
B	FIND	ARMOR	SWORDS	FOUR	THEY
C	ALLOW	THIRTY-ONE	FIVE	CAN	WEAR
D	TRIDENT	IT	BOWS	RUN	NOW

1. **Alex says**, "Cross off words that are numbers."

2. **Alex says**, "Cross off words that rhyme with *cow* or *moo*."

3. Cross off all nouns (people, places, things).

4. **Alex says**, "Cross off verbs (action words) in rows A and D."

5. **Alex says**, "Cross off Minecraft weapons in columns 1 and 3."

6. **Alex says**, "Read the remaining words to reveal something you should know about zombies."

Secret tip: _____

_____

WHEEL OF FORTUNE #2

Start at the ▼. Write every third letter on the spaces to reveal a fortune you want to claim.

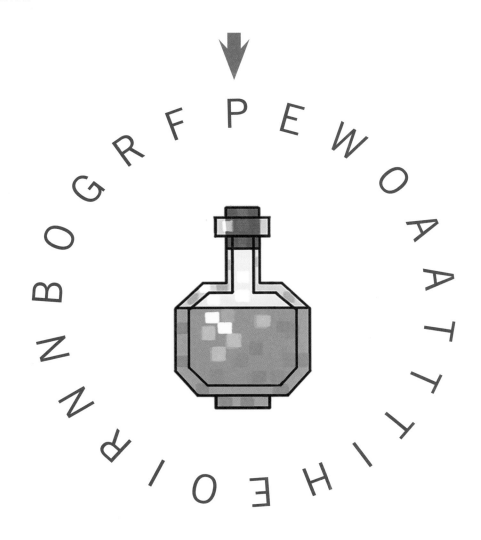

_ _ _ _ _ _ _ _ _ _ _ _ _ _ _ _

_ _ _ _ _ _ _

SADDLE SEARCH

Can you find the saddle? It appears spelled correctly only once in a horizontal, vertical, or diagonal line.

```
E   S   A   D   D   E   L   A   E   S
L   D   L   S   A   S   E   D   L   A
D   S   E   A   E   S   D   A   D   D
D   A   L   D   D   A   L   E   D   E
S   L   D   S   S   E   L   S   D   L
A   A   D   L   D   D   A   D   A   S
S   L   A   D   A   S   L   D   S   D
D   S   S   S   D   A   D   S   L   A
E   L   D   A   S   L   S   D   A   S
E   D   D   A   E   S   A   D   D   L
```

MEMO FROM MIRROR

Circle letters on the top half of the grid that have correct mirror images on the bottom half. Write the circled letters in order on the spaces to reveal a helpful tip.

```
W  H  E  D  O  N  O  R  U  T  S  L  V  E  B  C  E  P  O  N

A  B  E  O  J  D  I  N  M  T  S  Z  H  E  N  L  A  E  T  H

E  R  I  K  T  W  I  L  E  L  E  X  K  P  L  Y  O  D  E  G
```

```
Ǝ  Я  I  A  T  M  I  T  Ⅎ  Ǝ  X  X  Ʞ  Ⅎ  T  O  D  E  D

A  B  E  Ɔ  Ԁ  D  I  N  W  T  Z  И  H  E  И  I  Λ  E  T  H

W  A  T  D  O  N  O  Ԁ  И  T  S  ⅃  A  E  Ԁ  D  E  Ԁ  O  И
```

__ ___ __ ____ __ ___

__ ___ _____.

__ ____ _____.

SQUARED UP: LET THERE BE LIGHT

Each of the four light sources in this puzzle can appear only once in each row, column, and the four inside boxes. Can you fill each empty box below with the correct letter?

 B = BEACON

 G = GLOWSTONE

 L = LAVA

 T = TORCH

B			L
	T	G	
	L	B	
T			G

COOKIE FEAST

It's an all-you-can-eat cookie maze! Your job is to eat every single cookie. To do this, draw a line from Start to Stop that passes through every cookie once. Your line can go up, down, left, or right but not diagonally. On your mark, get set, munch!

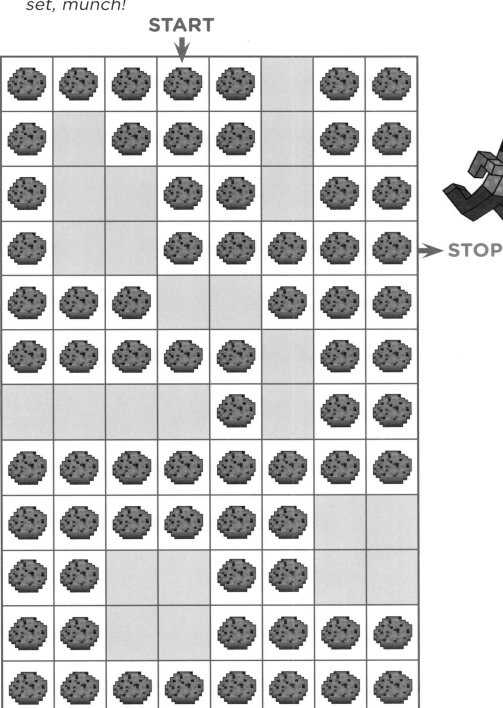

YOU CAN DRAW IT: WITCH

Use the grid to copy the picture. Examine each small square in the top grid, then transfer those lines to the corresponding square on the bottom grid.

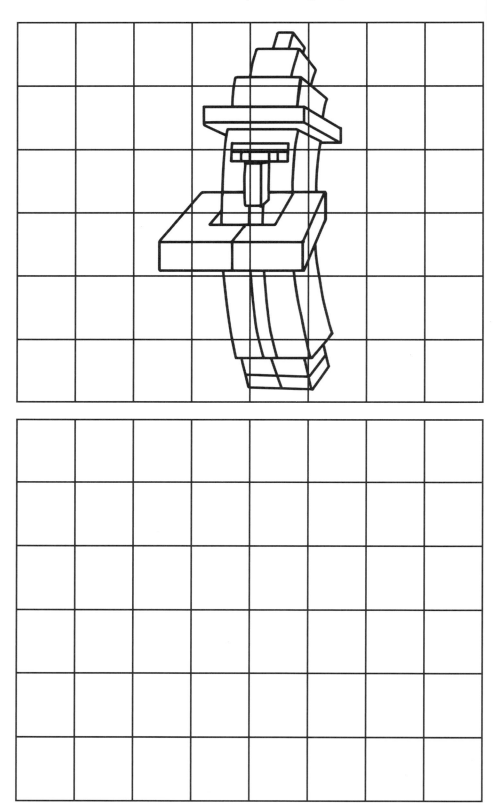

ENCHANTED BOOK

This book is enchanted. To open it and use it, you must press all nine buttons just once, in the correct order.

Follow the directions on the buttons. For instance, 2D means you must move your finger two buttons down. R=right, L=left, U=up. To open the book, you must land on the F button last.

Which button do you have to press first to land on the F button last?

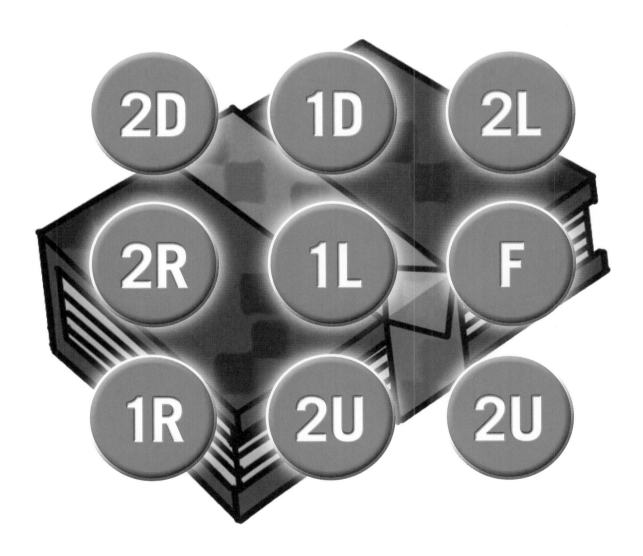

LONG LAUGH

The answer is written below. Read it.

Hint: *It helps to hold the page at eye level and shut one eye.*

What did the skeleton bring to the mob potluck picnic?

GETTIN' CRAFTY

Find and circle the names of nine things you craft in Minecraft. They might be forward, backward, up, down, or diagonal. Write unused letters on the spaces, in order from top to bottom and left to right, to reveal a tenth thing you can craft.

Hint: Circle individual letters instead of the whole word at once. The first one has been done for you.

BANNER	COOKIE	SHIELD
BEACON	HELMET	~~SHOVEL~~
BUCKET	LADDER	STRING

A S H O V E L B

R T C E A R R U

E R D O L B T C

D I O L A M O K

D N N N E O E E

 A G N A K I S T

L E T I I C H K

R B E A C O N S

_ _ _ _ _ _ _ _ _ _ _ _ _

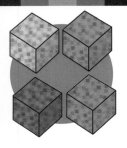

TRUE OR FALSE?

Find your way through this maze from Start to Finish. It will be easier if you answer the questions correctly.

START

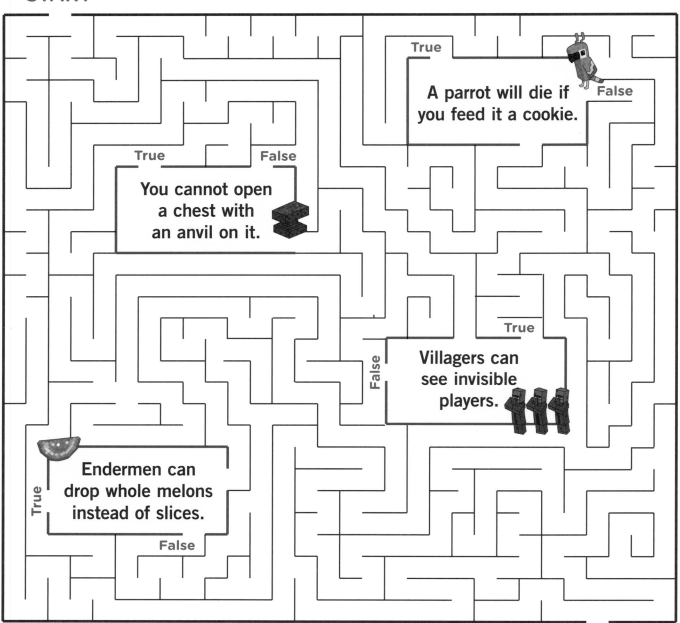

True

A parrot will die if you feed it a cookie.

False

True — False

You cannot open a chest with an anvil on it.

True

Villagers can see invisible players.

False

True

Endermen can drop whole melons instead of slices.

False

STOP

GO WITH THE FLOW CHART

Follow the instructions in the flow chart to reveal one of the most exciting things you can build in Minecraft. Do you know how to build this?

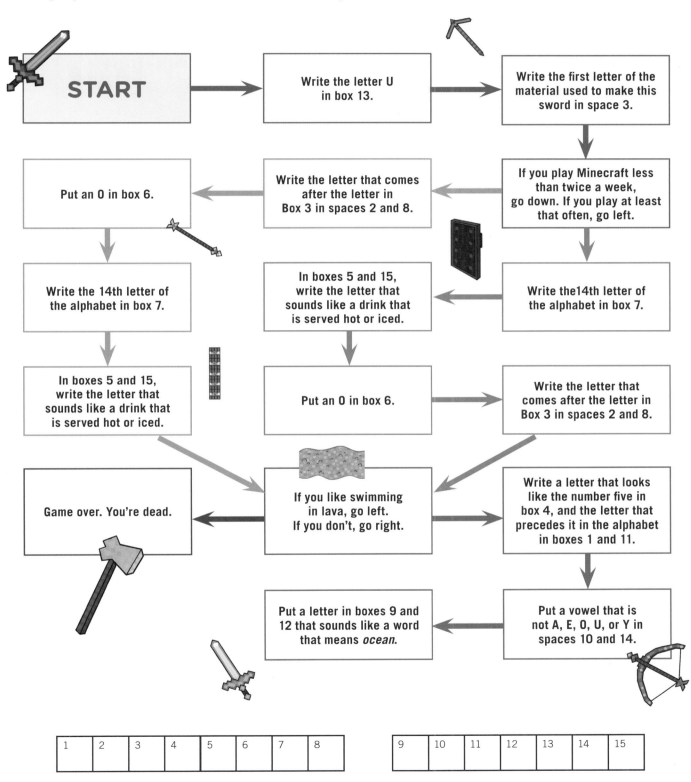

START

Write the letter U in box 13.

Write the first letter of the material used to make this sword in space 3.

Put an 0 in box 6.

Write the letter that comes after the letter in Box 3 in spaces 2 and 8.

If you play Minecraft less than twice a week, go down. If you play at least that often, go left.

Write the 14th letter of the alphabet in box 7.

In boxes 5 and 15, write the letter that sounds like a drink that is served hot or iced.

Write the14th letter of the alphabet in box 7.

In boxes 5 and 15, write the letter that sounds like a drink that is served hot or iced.

Put an 0 in box 6.

Write the letter that comes after the letter in Box 3 in spaces 2 and 8.

Game over. You're dead.

If you like swimming in lava, go left. If you don't, go right.

Write a letter that looks like the number five in box 4, and the letter that precedes it in the alphabet in boxes 1 and 11.

Put a letter in boxes 9 and 12 that sounds like a word that means *ocean*.

Put a vowel that is not A, E, O, U, or Y in spaces 10 and 14.

1	2	3	4	5	6	7	8

9	10	11	12	13	14	15

INSIDE INFO

Use the key to reveal a fun feature in Minecraft. Then use the key to decipher what you might call this feature.

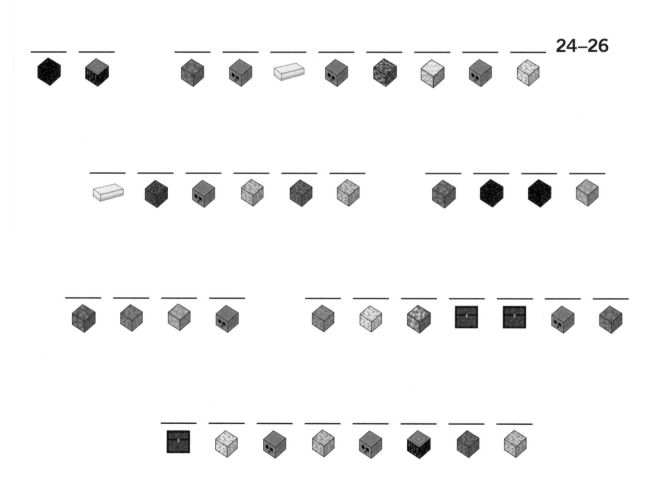

CREEPER DESTROYERS

Each of the five players below destroyed a different number of creepers (with five being the maximum). The numbers in the circles give you a hint. They show how many creepers were killed by both players whose squares touch the number. Use your addition facts to figure out how many creepers each player destroyed.

Hint: Do Xavier last!

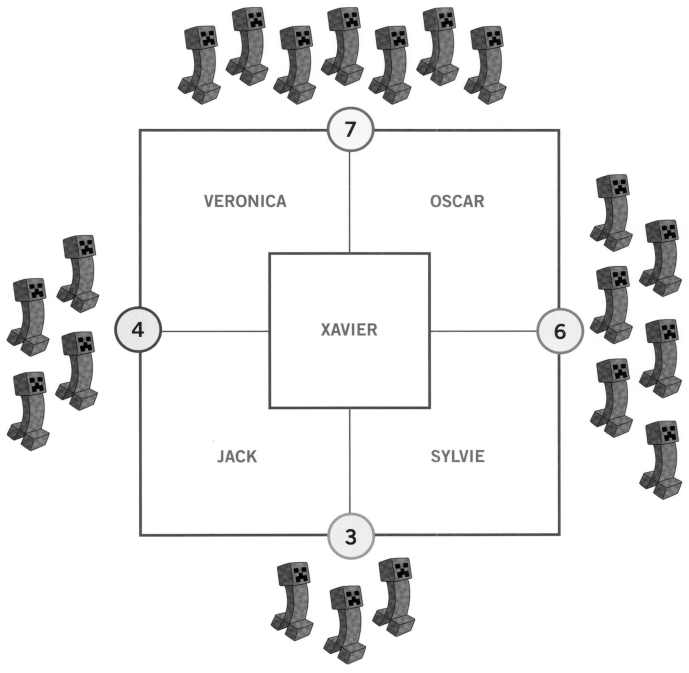

WHOOPS!

The answers to the clues use each letter in the letter box. Write the answers to the clues on the numbered spaces Then transfer the letters to the boxes with the same numbers. If you fill in the boxes correctly, you'll reveal the answer to the joke.

A A E N N P R S S T T

Material that hangs below
a basketball hoop

___ ___ ___
3   2   4

Resting sessions for babies

___ ___ ___ ___
5   6   7   8

A glowing ball of gas visible
in the sky at night

___ ___ ___ ___
9 10 11 12

**What did Alex get when she accidentally splashed
her mom and dad with a Potion of Invisibility?**

10	12	6	5	8	7	11	12	2	3	4	9

WHAT'S FOR DINNER?

Use the clues to figure out what each player eats to restore saturation and hunger levels.

YUM!

YUM!

- A zombie dropped Enderslayer's dinner.

- Of these four players, 4321Blastoff gets the most hunger points from her meal.

- Neither Emperor Nethero nor 4321Blastoff ate something yellow; either Enderslayer or Call me Fishmale ate something orange.

- Call me Fishmale's dinner is not grown as a crop, but Enderslayer's is.

- Either Emperor Nethero or Call me Fishmale caught his dinner while fishing.

YUM!

	ROTTEN FLESH	PUFFERFISH	POTATO	CARROT
Emperor Nethero				
Call me Fishmale				
Enderslayer				
4321Blastoff				

SCORE MORE ORE

It's a mining bonanza! To find your way through this maze, pick up six blocks each of iron ore, lapis lazuli, and redstone.

You must pick up your first block in the top row and your last block in the bottom row, and you must pick them up in this order:

Moving only up, down, left, and right, what path must you take?

TRADING JO(S)

Four Minecraft players, who all go by "Jo," are trading with villagers. Who is trading with whom?

To find out, begin at the dot below each player's name and follow it downward. Every time you hit a horizontal line (one that goes across), you must take it. See where each player's path leads.

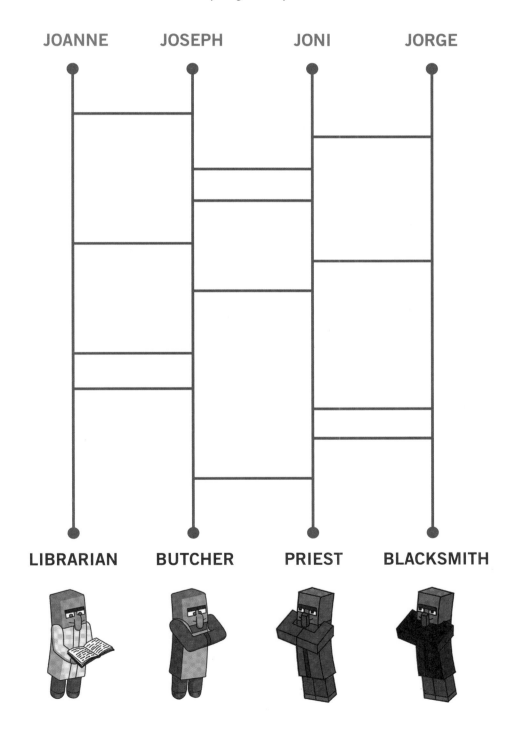

JOANNE   JOSEPH   JONI   JORGE

LIBRARIAN   BUTCHER   PRIEST   BLACKSMITH

THE LOCKED DOOR

Four players are racing to find the end portal that works. Follow each player's path, under and over crossing paths, to the portal they encounter, then follow the path from there to see whose portal leads to the Ender dragon.

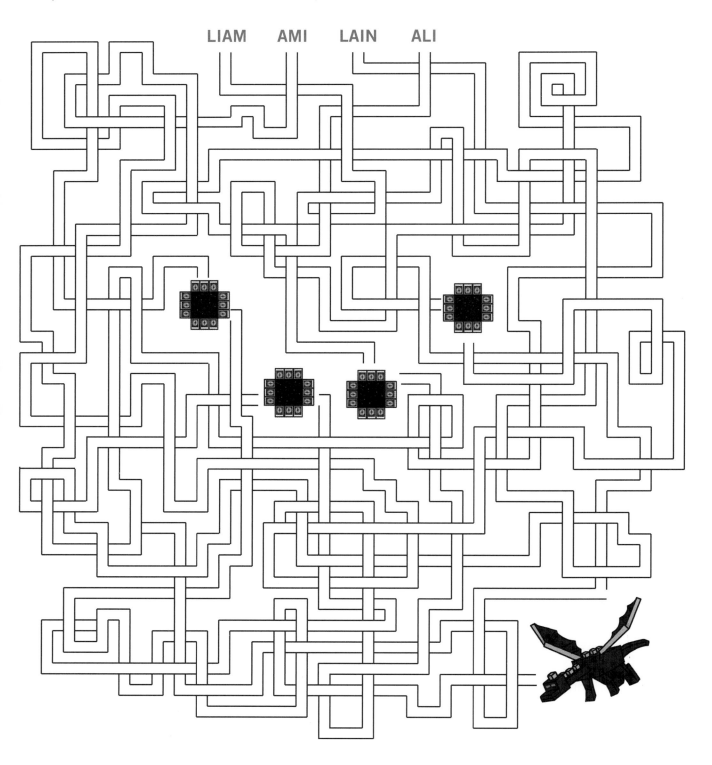

LIAM   AMI   LAIN   ALI

ZOMBIE FRIENDS

In this crossword, you get to figure out where each word fits! Use the picture clues to guess the word answers, then see where each word fits best. If you fill in the puzzle correctly, you'll discover the answer to the joke.

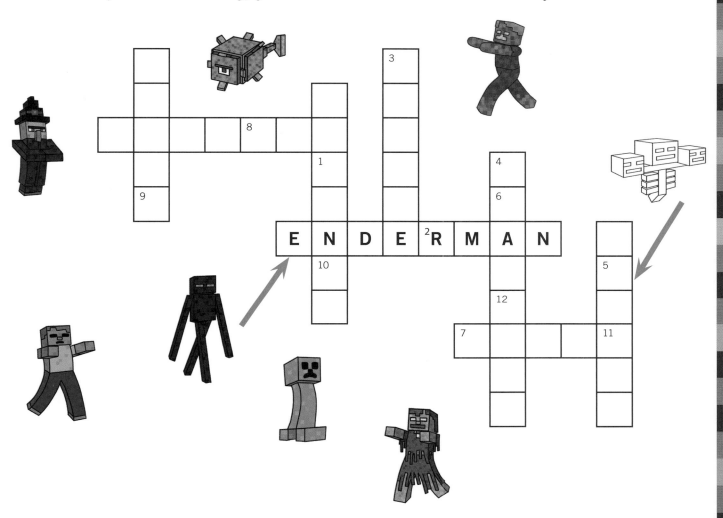

What did the zombie's friends say when he introduced his girlfriend?

_ _ _ _ , _ _ _ _ _ _ _ _ _ _ _
4 10 10 3   7 11 10 2 10   12 5 12   9 1 6

_ _ _ _ _ _ _ _ ?
12 5 4   11 10 2   6 8

ALEX SAYS: OWN YOUR MINE BUSINESS

If you have ever played the game Simon Says, then you know how this game works: follow only the directions that begin with "Alex says" to reveal a mining tip.

	1	2	3	4	5
A	A	SPIDER EYE	CAKE	SPOT	LOCATE
B	UNDER	FIND	GLASS BOTTLE	DISCOVER	DIAMONDS
C	DEEP	ACHE	IN	LAYER	STEAK
D	AND	TWELVE	OF	REDSTONE DUST	AGAIN

1. **Alex says**, "Cross off words that begin with vowels in column 1 and row D."

2. Cross off words that have two of the same letter.

3. **Alex says**, "Cross off items that are commonly dropped by witches."

4. **Alex says**, "Cross off words that mean *find* in columns four and five."

5. **Alex says**, "Cross off words that rhyme with *break*."

6. **Alex says**, "Read the remaining words to reveal a mining tip."

Mining tip: _____

_____

WHEEL OF FORTUNE #3

Start at the ↓.
Write every third letter on the spaces to reveal a treasure you want to claim.

_ _ _ _ _ _ _ _ _ _ _ _ _ _ _ _

_ _ _ _ _ _ _ _ _ _

HIDDEN ARMOR

Can you find the phrase "horse armor"? It appears spelled correctly only once in a horizontal, vertical, or diagonal line.

```
M R H O R S E A R M O H
A O O R M R A S R O H S
H O R S E A R M R O A E
O E S S R O M S R O H O
R H E A E R E S A S M M
S R O M R A E S R O H R
E S A O H A R M A O O A
A E R E R O M E R S M E
R O M M H S S S M A E S
R H O A E R E S R O H R
O O R R O M R A E S R O
R A M H R A E S R O H H
```

REFLECTIONS IN THE WATER

Circle letters on the bottom half of the grid that have correct mirror images in the top half. Write the circled letters in order on the spaces to reveal a weapon tip.

R O M P H T R I I D E N C T B A K C K F S

M E N T B C K R I N G S S Y O U E A R T H

S A H I L O P A Y L T M R Y E N C H E A N T

Z A V T L O R Y A L T M K Y E N C H B A N T

M E N T B G X R I N G S N N Y O U D B R T H

R O W L N T R I J D E N O T B A X C K I B Z

__ __ __ __ __ __ __ __ __ __ __ __ __ __

__ __ __ __ __ __ __ __

__ __ __ __ __ __

SQUARED UP: LOGICAL LOOT

Each loot item below is found just once in each column, each row, and each of the four inner boxes. B represents bone, R represents rotten flesh, and so on. Can you fill every empty square with the right letter?

 B = BONE

 R = ROTTEN FLESH

 S = STICK

 W = WATER BOTTLE

	B		W
R			
			S
W		B	

FLOWERS TO DYE FOR

Your job is to make the most dye possible. That means collecting every flower in this maze. To do this, draw a line from Start to Stop that passes through every flower once. Your line can go up, down, left, or right but not diagonally. On your mark, get set, gather!

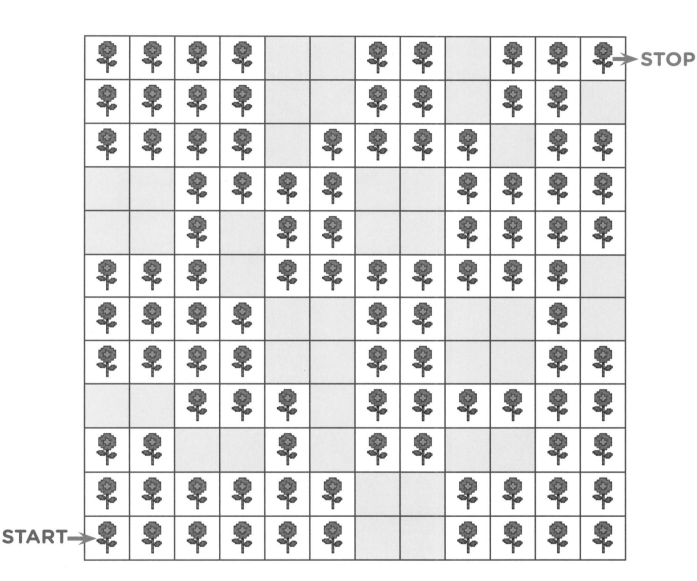

START→

→STOP

SHIP SHAPE

Boxes connected by lines contain the same letter. Some letters are given; others have to be guessed. Fill in all the boxes to reveal some of the cool things about the Update Aquatic. Then transfer the letters in the numbered boxes to the spaces with the same numbers to reveal the answer to the joke.

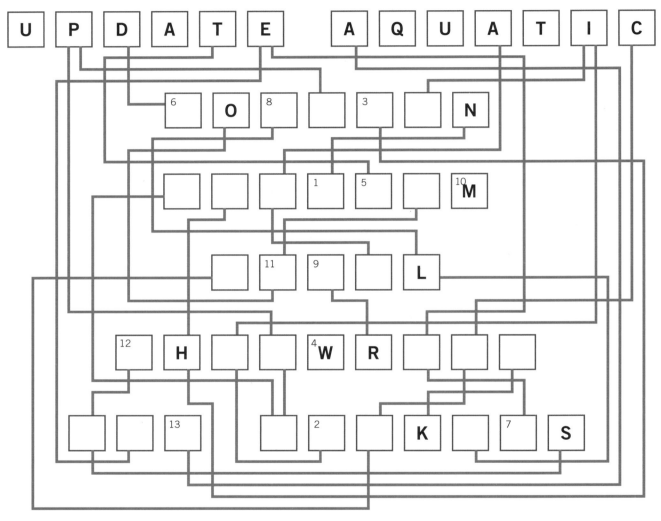

U P D A T E   A Q U A T I C

What happened in the wreck between the red ship and the blue ship?

___ ___ ___   ___ ___ ___ ___ ___ ___ ___
5   3   7   12 13 2   8   11 9   12

___ ___ ___ ___   ___ ___ ___ ___ ___ ___ ___
4   7   9   7   10 13 9   11 11 1   7   6

ENCHANTED TRAP DOOR

This trap door is enchanted. To open it, you must press all twelve buttons just once, in the correct order.

Follow the directions on the buttons. For instance, 2D means you must move your finger two buttons down. R=right, L=left, U=up. To open the trap door, you must land on the F button last.

Which button do you have to press first to land on the F button last?

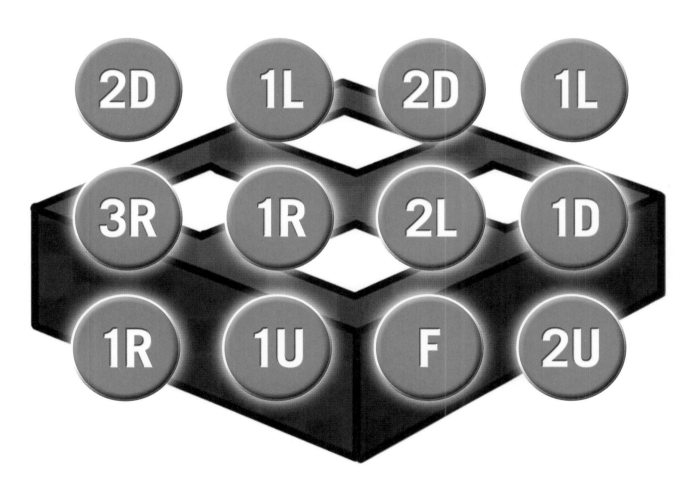

TALL TALE

Did you hear about the famous skeleton artist?

There's a funny answer to this question, and it's hidden in the lines below. See if you can read it.

Hint: It helps to hold the page at eye level and shut one eye.

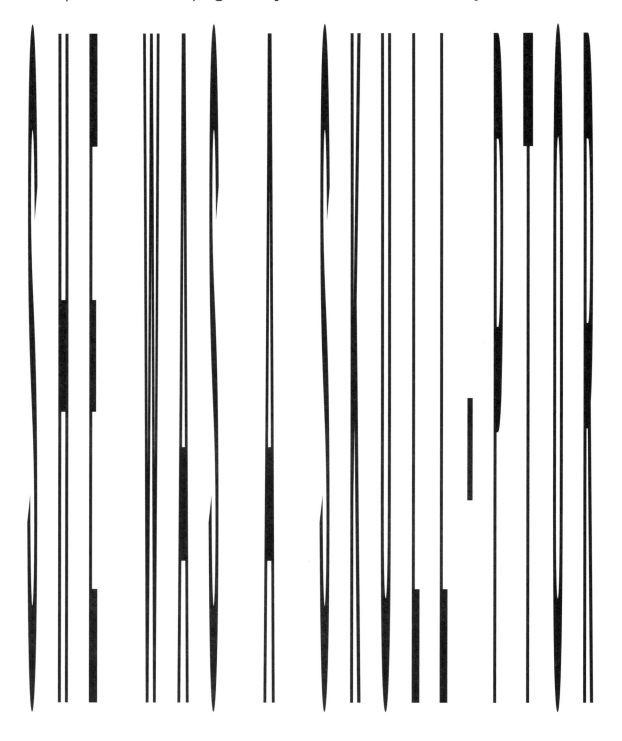

ANIMALS, ANIMALS EVERYWHERE

Find and circle the names of 17 animals in the wordfind. They might be forward, backward, up, down, or diagonal. Write unused letters on the blank spaces, in order from top to bottom and left to right, to discover a tip for protecting crops from animals.

Hint: Circle individual letters instead of whole words. We've found one to get you started.

```
S  B  H  U  Y  E  K  N  O  D  E  I
A  P  L  O  D  A  L  D  I  L  R  S
L  T  U  I  R  T  S  L  U  L  P  D
M  A  N  F  O  S  D  M  A  I  I  O
O  W  O  L  F  N  E  A  D  M  L  L
N  A  E  T  K  E  E  E  T  O  A  P
G  C  P  O  L  A  R  B  E  A  R  H
O  R  O  R  W  A  S  F  T  E  P  I
A  T  U  R  T  L  E  D  I  Y  E  N
S  U  P  A  D  I  U  Q  S  S  E  P
L  Y  O  P  F  N  E  K  C  I  H  C
W  H (R  A  B  B  I  T) E  A  S  T
```

CHICKEN
DOLPHIN
DONKEY
HORSE
LLAMA
MULE
OCELOT
PARROT
POLAR BEAR
PUFFERFISH
~~RABBIT~~
SALMON
SHEEP
SPIDER
SQUID
TURTLE
WOLF

_ _ _ _ _ _   _   _ _ _ _   _ _ _ _ _ _   _ _ _

_   _ _ _ _   _   _ _ _ _   _   _ _ _ _ _ _

_ _ _ _ _ _ _ _   _ _   _ _ _ _ _

LETTER HUNT

Identify the shared letter in each group of four words. Only one letter is in all four words. Write that shared letter on the space provided, then transfer the letters from the spaces to the boxes with the same numbers. If you fill in the boxes correctly, you'll earn a rare reward.

1. ____	TROPICAL, BEHAVIOR, MINECART, GHAST
2. ____	PUFFERFISH, HOSTILE, PHANTOM, ACHIEVEMENT
3. ____	PLAYERS, REDSTONE, TRANSPARENT, ANIMALS
4. ____	PASSIVE, TAMEABLE, MECHANISM, SILVERFISH
5. ____	ENDERMITE, UTILITY, MOUNTAIN, COBBLESTONE
6. ____	INVENTORY, FLOWER, CREATIVE, DRAGON
7. ____	PRISMARINE, DISPENSER, GUARDIAN, SPAWN

7	4	5	2	4	6

3	5	1	6

MATH MOBS

The numbers at the end of the rows are linked to the images in the grid.

What number goes in the circle?

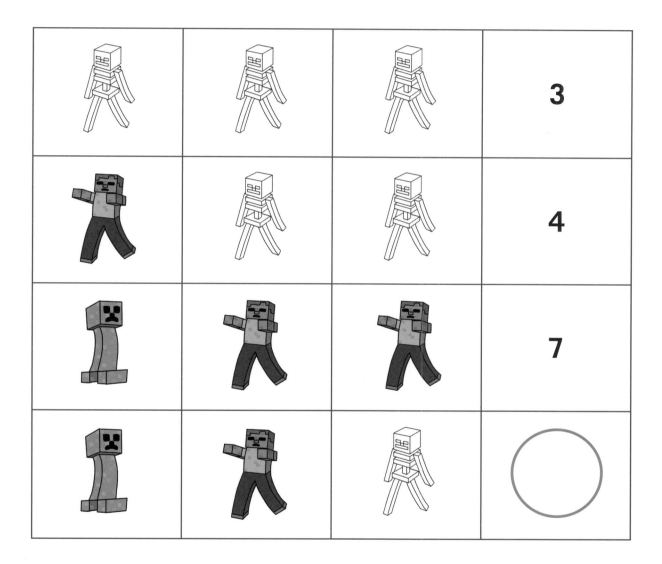

SO MUCH FOR PEACEFUL!

Use the key to reveal something you'll want to watch out for even when playing in peaceful mode.

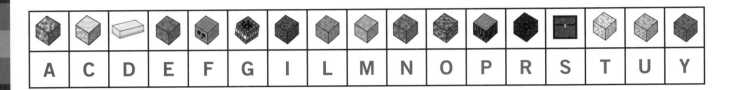

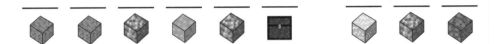

BABY'S FAVORITE TOY

Every word in Column B contains the same letters as a word in Column A, plus one letter. Draw a line between word "matches," then write the extra letter on the space provided. Transfer the numbered letters from the column to the spaces at the bottom to discover the answer to the joke.

COLUMN A	COLUMN B	
Stored	Redstone	___ 1
Groan	Wither	___ 2
Canoe	Layer	___ 3
White	Dragon	___ 4
Snorted	Destroy	___ 5
Rely	Beacon	___ 6

What is a baby zombie's favorite toy?

___ ___ ___ ___ ___ ___   ___ ___ ___ ___
3   4   1   3   4   5   6   1   3   2

HIDDEN HAZARD

Uncover the danger in the grid, if you dare. Color every box that has an even number, and be prepared to protect yourself.

Can't see the danger? Try turning the page on its side and holding it in front of a mirror.

72	46	20	16	4	32	64	88
29	98	54	23	21	11	83	23
41	63	67	30	2	65	13	49
35	7	93	47	61	68	18	27
50	78	26	90	74	10	82	6
25	97	59	31	47	5	15	61
53	12	70	82	22	46	38	3
34	89	71	19	79	95	53	18
56	75	39	1	29	71	95	66
5	66	72	38	16	8	44	23
17	45	67	85	35	47	59	35
55	36	16	94	3	20	52	57
80	13	27	14	25	65	83	34
48	11	15	91	51	37	51	98
33	64	58	20	6	78	82	81
21	71	85	5	45	93	57	43
52	68	18	90	13	43	1	63
69	9	97	42	76	82	34	77
1	33	31	98	7	49	29	50
73	27	15	16	90	66	32	85
8	84	56	62	55	45	9	21
17	61	91	87	73	37	11	69
44	6	79	37	74	26	8	41
81	55	30	14	51	77	99	22
89	57	65	98	41	15	63	78
96	18	76	28	50	32	96	46
33	7	39	53	17	99	3	31
43	20	56	2	48	22	70	87
4	25	67	59	67	19	9	62
16	49	39	3	19	75	19	88
38	42	66	18	30	24	96	72

WHOSE BIOME IS THIS?

Use the clues to figure out where each player is exploring.

- Either MineQueen or ZipDooDa should watch out for guardians.

- Knowitall says, "Llamas and emerald ore occur naturally here."

- Squ88mish is looking at a blue terracotta block inside a sandstone structure or a squid.

- MineQueen is not in a place to harvest cocoa pods, and neither is Knowitall.

- ZipDooDa sees a parrot or a fossil.

	MOUNTAINS	DESERT	DEEP OCEAN	JUNGLE
Squ88mish				
MineQueen				
ZipDooDa				
Knowitall				

MOB DROPS

Draw a line between the mob and the item it drops when destroyed. No diagonal lines allowed. No two lines will cross or share a square. If you do it correctly, no two lines will cross or share a square.

Example:

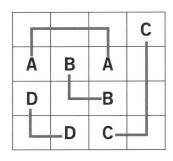

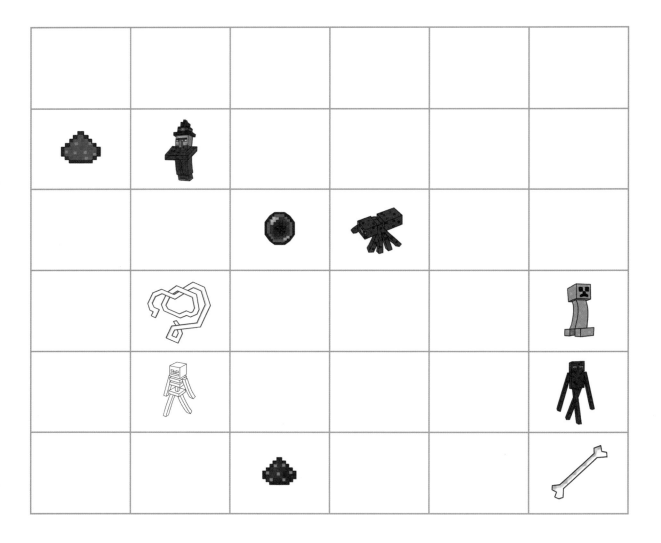

SURPRISE!

Four Minecraft players accidentally trip a wire that opens a door and reveals a surprise. Three players get harmless surprises, but one gets a dangerous surprise. Which player gets which surprise?

To find out, begin at the dot below each player's name and follow it downward. Every time you hit a horizontal line (one that goes across), you must take it. See where each player's path leads.

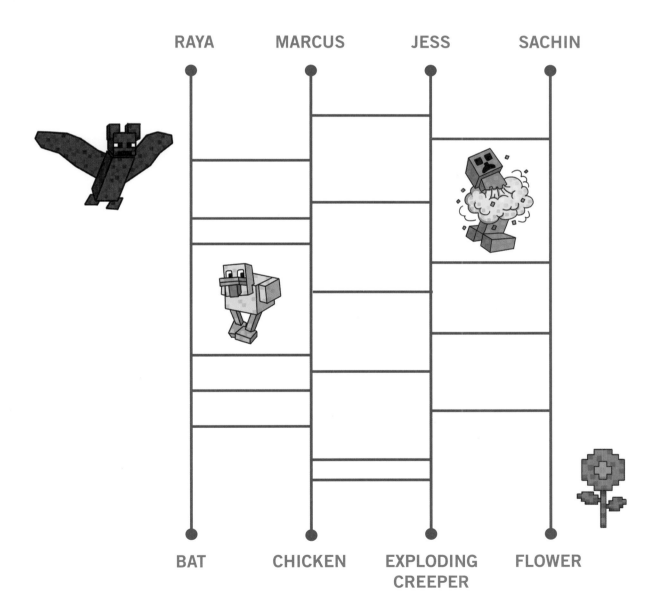

RAYA   MARCUS   JESS   SACHIN

BAT   CHICKEN   EXPLODING CREEPER   FLOWER

YOU CAN DRAW IT: CREEPER FAMILY

Use the grid to copy the picture. Examine each small square in the top grid, then transfer those lines to the corresponding square on the bottom grid.

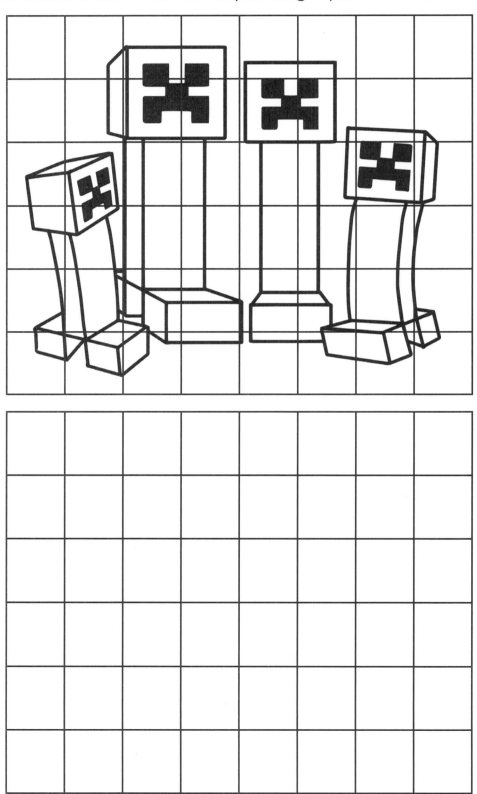

WHAT ZOMBIES WANT

In this crossword, you get to figure out where each word fits! Use the picture clues to guess the word answers, then see where each word fits best. If you fill in the puzzle correctly, you'll discover the answer to the joke.

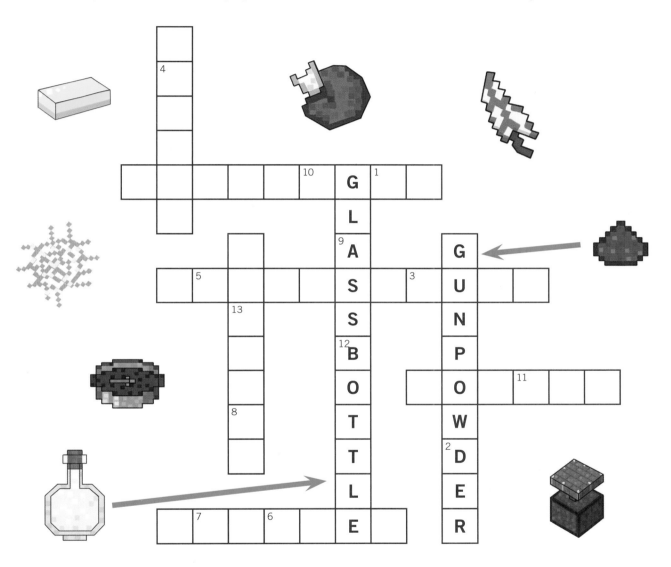

Why did the zombie attack the skeleton?

‾‾ ‾‾   ‾‾ ‾‾ ‾‾ ‾‾ ‾‾ ‾‾   ‾‾ ‾‾ ‾‾
4 6   11 9 10 6 7 2   5 4 8

‾‾ ‾‾ ‾‾ ‾‾   ‾‾ ‾‾ ‾‾   ‾‾ ‾‾ ‾‾ ‾‾ ‾‾ ‾‾
12 1 10 7   9 10 2   13 9 3 3 1 11

WHODUNNIT?

Two mobs have done you serious damage. Recover full health by figuring out whodunnit.

Write the name of the pictured mob on the spaces. Use the fractions to circle one or more of the letters in the name. Transfer the circled letters to the boxes to reveal whodunnit. We've done the first one for you.

LAST ⅕ OF		1. P U F F E R F I (S H)
MIDDLE ½ OF		2. __ __ __ __ __
LAST ½ OF		3. __ __ __ __ __ __ __ __
FIRST ⅕ OF		4. __ __ __ __ __ __
FIRST ⅔ OF		5. __ __ __
SECOND ¼ OF		6. __ __ __ __ __ __ __ __ __
MIDDLE ⅕ OF		7. __ __ __ __ __ __

¹S	H	²		³				⁴	⁵		⁶		⁷	

WHEEL OF FORTUNE #4

Start at the ▼.
Write every third letter on the spaces to reveal something simple with a super-impressive name.

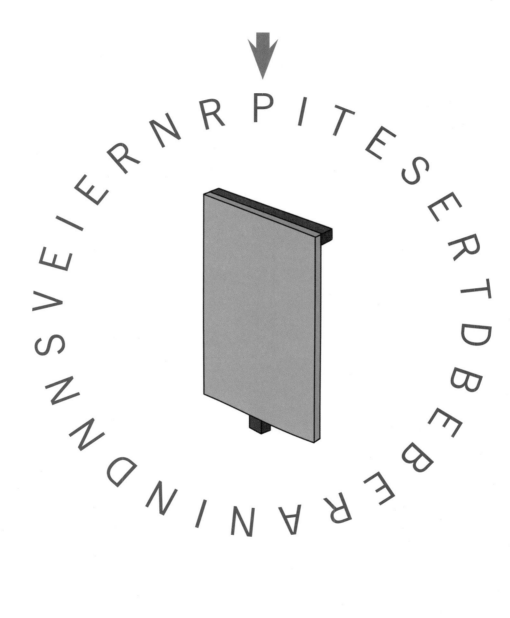

_ _ _   _ _ _   _ _ _ _ _ _ _

_ _ _ _ _ _ _ _   _ _ _ _ _

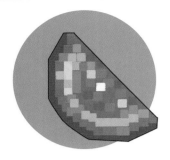

SEED FINDER

Can you find the melon seeds? They appear only once in a horizontal, vertical, or diagonal line.

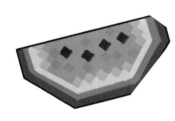

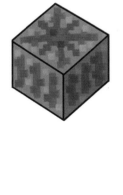

```
M O S E E S N O L E M S
E E D M E L O N S E D N
L M E O M S L E L E M O
O M E L E E N O E S L L
N E N L E D N M S D E E
S L O S O S E E E O M N
E O L O E N O E N L O O
E N E E E L S E M E N L
S E M O N O L E E M S E
L S S D E E S N E L E M
O N M E L O N S E D D O
N D S S E N O L E M S L
```

IN THE BEGINNING . . .

Circle letters on the bottom half of the grid that have correct mirror images in the top half. Write the circled letters in order on the spaces to reveal a behind-the-scenes fact about Minecraft.

E Π T O B ⅄ E O B Ɔ I Ɔ ∀ D Ɯ Ɔ E И

Γ Ɔ Ⅎ ⅄ Ɔ Ƨ H E W O T B T Ƨ Ɯ E D Я

O Ɯ Я I Ɔ ∀ K I И ∀ Γ B Ƨ Ɯ Γ ∀ Ɔ ϽI

———————————————————————————

O W R I G A R I N A L E S N L Y O U V I

L C J L A G S M E M O L B I S W E B P R

E A L T O B X E G F P D I G A C M O E N

_ _ _ _ _ _ _ _ _ _ _ , _ _ _ _ _ _ _

_ _ _ _ _ _

_ _ _ _ _ _ _ _ _ _

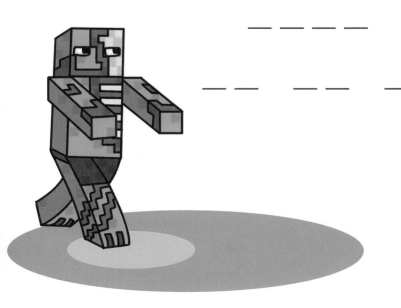

YOU CAN DRAW IT: ENDERDRAGON

Use the grid to copy the picture. Examine each small square in the top grid, then transfer those lines to the corresponding square on the bottom grid.

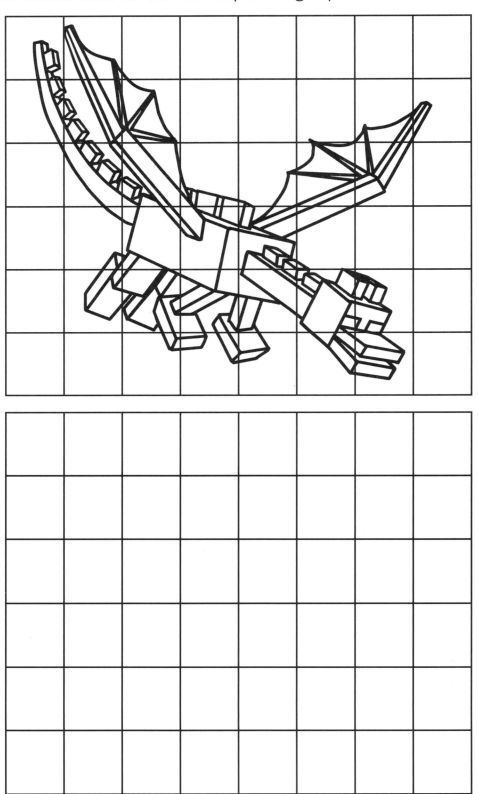

BOUNTIFUL HARVEST

You will soon head out on an adventure. You need all the food in your inventory that you can collect. That means picking up every edible item in this maze. To do this, draw a line from Start to Stop that passes through every piece of food once. Your line can go up, down, left, or right but not diagonally. On your mark, get set, stock up!

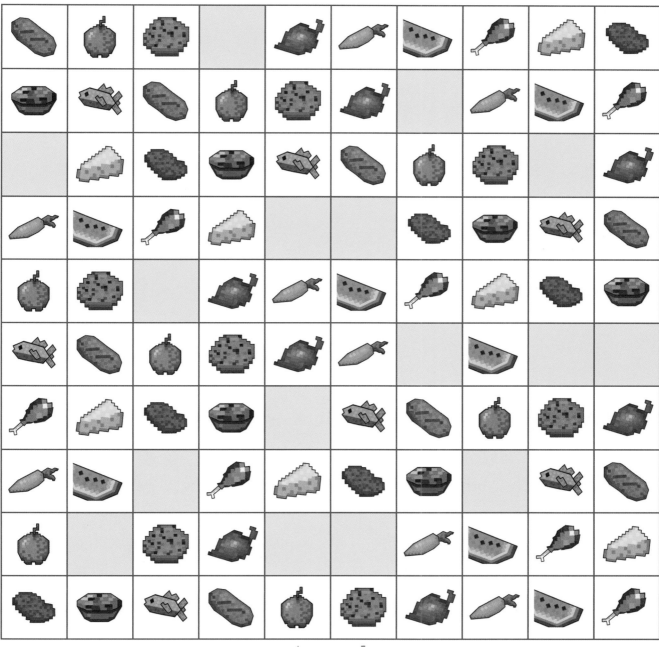

START STOP

NAME SHIFTING

Follow the instructions to transform this mob's name to its nickname.

1. Write the **name of this mob** on the space to the right.	
2. Move **the second vowel** to the end of the name.	
3. Change the **middle two letters** of the name to the first two letters of the alphabet.	
4. Change the **second letter** of the name to something that when combined with the first letter, it makes a sound that means "be quiet."	
5. Make the **first letter** the fourth letter in the name, and change it to the fourth letter of the alphabet.	
6. Make the **first half** of the name swap positions with the second half of the name.	

ENCHANTED BOW AND ARROW

The bow and arrow are enchanted. To use them, you must press all sixteen buttons just once, in the correct order.

Follow the directions on the buttons. For instance, 2D means you must move your finger two buttons down. R = right, L = left, U = up. To use the bow and arrow, you must land on the F button last.

Which button do you have to press first to land on the F button last?

3D	2D	1L	2D
1R	2R	1R	2D
2U	1R	1D	3L
2U	F	2U	3U

WHICH WITCH?

What do you call a witch that spawns in the desert?

The answer is written below. Read it.

Hint: It helps to hold the page at eye level and shut one eye.

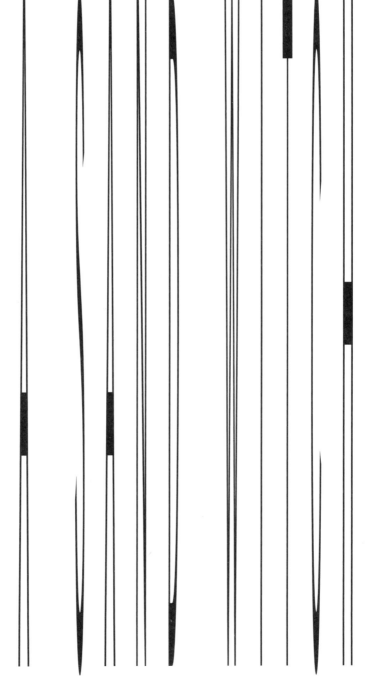

PICK A POTION

Find and circle the names of 14 potions in the wordfind. They might be forward, backward, up, down, or diagonal. Write unused letters on the blank spaces, in order from top to bottom and left to right, to discover something useful to know.

Hint: Circle individual letters instead of whole words. We've found one to get you started.

ANTIDOTE
DECAY
ELIXIR
EYEDROPS
HEALING
INVISIBILITY
NIGHT VISION
POISON
REGENERATION
~~SLOWNESS~~
STRENGTH
SWIFTNESS
TONIC
TURTLE MASTER

A N I S H E A L I N G R
I N N S T T Y A C E D E
A N V T D R A M A T G T
S W I F T N E S S O E S
I V S C P L O N T D I A
N O I S I V T H G I N M
O N B X C N A N K T I E
L L I A O P O L A N H L
Y R L S E R A T T A O T
N O I T A R E N E G E R
N O T S L O W N E S S U
P E Y E D R O P S C E T

__ __   __ __ __ __ __ __   __ __ __ __ __   __ __

__ __ __ __ __ __   __ __   __ __ __ __

__ __   __ __ __ __ __ __   __ __   __ __ __ __

TEXT STRINGS

Identify the shared letter in each group of four words. Only one letter is in all four words. Write that shared letter on the space provided, then transfer the letters from the spaces to the boxes with the same numbers. If you fill in the boxes correctly, you'll reveal an advanced feature of Minecraft. Do you know how to use this feature?

3. ___	DIAMOND, SLIMEBALL, MULTIPLAYER, EXTREME
2. ___	BEETROOT, EXPLORER, PORKCHOP, PISTON
4. ___	ENVIRONMENT, FERMENTED, LUMINANCE, COMPARATOR
8. ___	COORDINATES, NAUTILUS, SLOWNESS, SHIPWRECK
7. ___	GUARDIAN, CAULDRON, WOODLAND, DESERT
5. ___	VINDICATOR, FURNACE, QUARTZ, MINESHAFT
6. ___	SKELETON, SWIFTNESS, INGREDIENT, OBSIDIAN
1. ___	RESISTANCE, MYCELIUM, TORCH, RECIPE

1	2	3	4	5	6	7	8

ADDITIONAL MATH MOBS

The numbers at the end of the rows and columns are linked to the images in the grid. What number goes in the circle?

Hint: Start with the column of pigs.

pig	cow	sheep	**11**
pig	cow	cow	**10**
pig	sheep	sheep	**12**
pig	sheep	pig	**9**
8	**18**	◯	

FLOWER POWER

Use the picture-number combination under each space to find the correct letter on the grid. The correct letter is the one where the picture and number intersect. If you fill in the spaces correctly, you'll discover a Minecrafting secret.

1	L	H	W	U	R
2	V	T	M	G	D
3	E	J	A	I	F
4	S	O	C	B	N

A RARE FIND

Every word in Column B contains the same letters as a word in Column A, plus one letter. Draw a line between word "matches," then write the extra letter on the space provided.

Unscramble the column of letters to reveal a rare find.

COLUMN A	COLUMN B	
Dasher	Hardcore	___
Yoked	Player	___
Early	Golem	___
Charred	Spider	___
Pride	Sheared	___
Mole	Donkey	___

What rare find did you just reveal?

__ __ __ __ __ __

MINER HUMOR

What do you get when you throw a piano down a mineshaft?

To find out, color every box that contains a multiple of five.

77	9	63	41	51	82	10	1	68	79	70	92	38	12	23	29	73	2	14	29
70	25	5	20	95	50	6	52	33	27	17	50	90	58	41	97	11	63	47	36
91	52	8	69	48	89	30	9	73	11	44	18	42	15	10	65	85	40	12	54
97	35	80	55	60	40	98	93	2	16	87	91	92	64	55	84	22	76	5	67
76	86	17	3	78	81	15	72	47	67	51	78	4	26	80	7	13	23	52	25
7	90	65	75	45	30	49	96	24	82	1	10	75	60	45	30	20	90	35	39
85	4	56	41	61	74	38	23	37	96	25	31	83	72	95	38	81	47	11	31
54	68	79	98	26	16	6	69	73	57	64	8	14	66	21	52	59	19	33	89
36	40	85	60	5	35	50	14	95	53	8	79	53	39	24	3	73	1	21	9
20	86	23	11	59	21	9	49	42	26	2	26	66	62	88	47	27	94	62	38
46	17	94	62	7	49	84	18	94	48	15	67	17	34	5	93	42	13	96	13
60	70	15	20	85	90	5	31	4	81	37	85	25	80	40	30	55	70	56	51
46	69	36	78	2	60	31	86	99	57	24	77	61	18	65	41	68	3	95	59
28	4	92	14	42	78	55	39	92	22	12	6	13	34	83	28	32	16	88	5
71	30	80	75	25	30	46	51	73	53	87	43	32	27	87	48	61	10	30	81
10	58	36	22	61	4	32	12	2	18	53	56	29	8	44	71	22	91	19	32
64	82	83	34	62	83	54	88	58	13	40	95	20	70	90	65	15	5	30	15
74	75	90	85	20	10	72	43	62	5	69	27	44	87	14	19	79	74	7	48
15	44	55	66	49	39	55	81	59	19	97	63	48	1	74	37	57	12	24	18
90	52	98	80	76	99	40	88	53	28	34	30	90	27	41	35	26	64	29	96
33	20	89	21	60	25	59	66	16	77	65	79	3	55	82	6	20	68	86	57
57	43	7	21	33	89	28	39	54	73	50	93	76	63	25	54	90	71	37	46
91	66	32	71	3	15	63	67	84	97	1	10	45	5	60	85	17	46	86	31
85	45	30	60	75	33	77	6	43	58	75	82	36	84	24	44	58	69	8	92
99	62	88	90	5	67	43	91	89	94	56	9	77	19	5	71	29	76	47	98
74	14	57	42	83	10	23	34	61	84	80	60	25	15	70	10	5	35	20	65
51	93	22	42	95	68	49	16	78	95	68	38	87	11	50	56	73	28	94	33

Can't read it? Try turning the page on its side.

DROP MATCH

Draw a line between the object and the item it drops when mined.
No diagonal lines allowed. No two lines will cross or share a square.

Example:

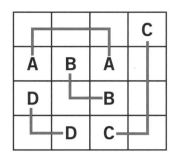

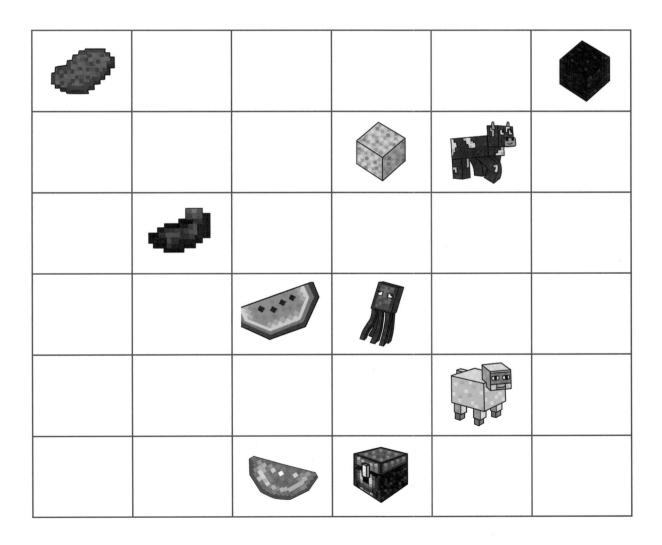

A COLD RECEPTION

The answers to the clues use each of the letters in the letter box. Write the answers to the clues on the numbered spaces Then transfer the letters to the boxes with the same numbers. If you fill in the boxes correctly, you'll reveal the answer to the joke.

$$\boxed{\text{B E F I O R S T T}}$$

A group of things that go together,
sometimes called a "matched ___"

<u> </u> <u> </u> <u> </u>
1   2   3

Lie

<u> </u> <u> </u> <u> </u>
4   5   6

Go bad, spoil

<u> </u> <u> </u> <u> </u>
7   8   9

What do you get from a hostile wolf in the Snowy Taiga?

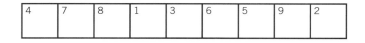

4	7	8	1	3	6	5	9	2

ANSWERS

PAGE 5 WHEEL OF FORTUNE #1

FORTUNE-ENCHANTED PICK

PAGE 6 ALEX SAYS: TOOL TIP

DON'T WASTE DIAMONDS ON A SHOVEL.

It may last longer, but there are better uses for diamonds.

PAGE 7 THE MIRROR'S MESSAGE

TO WORK, SPLASH POTIONS MUST HIT THE LOWER HALF OF A GHAST.

PAGE 9 SHOP AROUND THE BLOCK

THE GROSSERY STORE

PAGE 10 STAY AWAY!

LATER, PET, HORN

NETHER PORTAL

PAGE 11 ENCHANTED CHEST

F   2D   1L

1U   **1R**   1U

1U   1R   2L

The red button is the first one pressed.

PAGE 12 KILLER JOKE

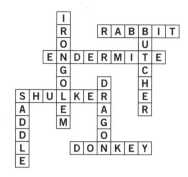

What's the difference between a killer rabbit and a counterfeit dollar bill?

ONE IS BAD MONEY AND THE OTHER IS A MAD BUNNY!

PAGE 13 GEM SEARCH

```
L A E D L E R E M E
E R A M E M A M D R
D M L D E E E L E A
A L E D L R A D M (D)
E L A R E M E E L D
M A D R A A D A E L
E L R D M L (R) E D A
R M D A R (E) L A L R
A E A L (M) A E D E E
D E M (E) R E D L A M
```

PAGE 14 BURIED TREASURE

		78		4	92		50		
44	10	70			18		16	28		14
26		62	56		66		38	60		32
12		8	74		30	2		54	32		6

PAGE 16 FAVORITE THING TO DO

Mohit - Battle mobs   Lu - Solve mazes

Jasmine - Build   Claire - Brew potions

PAGE 17 SQUARED UP: GARDEN PLOT

M	P	C	B
C	B	P	M
P	M	B	C
B	C	M	P

PAGE 18 HOMEWARD BOUND

START

STOP

PAGE 19 LIFE-SAVING STEPS

FAST ONES, AWAY FROM THE MOB!

PAGE 21 FACT OF (REAL) LIFE

P	H	O	S	P	H	O	R	U	S
Q	I	P	T	Q	I	P	S	V	T
R	J	Q	U	R	J	Q	T	W	U

	Z	M	C	
	A	N	D	
	B	O	E	

A	Y	J	A	G	S	K
B	Z	K	B	H	T	L
C	A	L	C	I	U	M

PAGE 22 MYSTERY MOB

GHAST

The ghast is real. Watch out for fireballs!

PAGE 23 NETHER FINDS

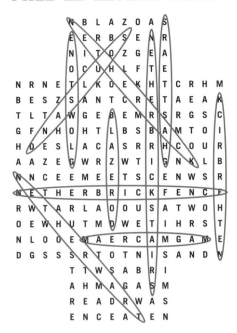

PAGE 24 WHO'S WHOSE ON THE FARM

BlockBuster - Pig

iBuild - Chicken

Creeper Hunter - Sheep

Masterminer - Donkey

PAGE 25 PARTY SNACK PICK-UP

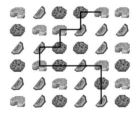

PAGE 26 GET OUT!

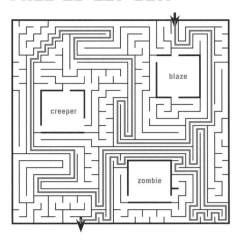

PAGE 28 WISHING YOU GOOD . . .

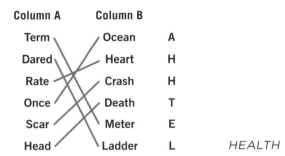

Column A	Column B	
Term	Ocean	A
Dared	Heart	H
Rate	Crash	H
Once	Death	T
Scar	Meter	E
Head	Ladder	L

HEALTH

PAGE 29 RARE DROP SCORES

Kim - *Ghast Tear*   Talia - *Nether Star*

Malik - *Blaze Rod*   Cameron - *Ender Pearls*

PAGE 30 LOST LIBRARY

MASH finds the library.

PAGE 31 UNCOMMON COMMON FEATURE

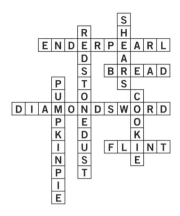

What do a librarian, priest, and nitwit have in common?

UNUSED HOODS ON THEIR ROBES.

It's true. You'll find hoods in their textures, but they aren't used.

PAGE 32 ALEX SAYS: DID YOU KNOW THIS ABOUT ZOMBIES?

IF ZOMBIES FIND ARMOR, THEY CAN WEAR IT.

So don't leave it lying around, okay?

PAGE 33 WHEEL OF FORTUNE #2

POTION OF WATER BREATHING

PAGE 34 SADDLE SEARCH

E S A D D E L A E S
L D L S A S E D L A
D S (E) A E S D A D D
D A (L) D D A L E D E
S L (D) S S E L S D L
A A (D) L D D A D A S
S L (A) D A S L D S D
D S (S) S D A D S L A
E L D A S L S D A S
E D D A E S A D D L

PAGE 35 MEMO FROM MIRROR

DO NOT SLEEP ON A BED IN THE NETHER. IT WILL EXPLODE.

PAGE 36 SQUARED UP: LET THERE BE LIGHT

B	G	T	L
L	T	G	B
G	L	B	T
T	B	L	G

PAGE 37 COOKIE FEAST

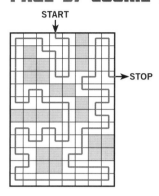

PAGE 39 ENCHANTED BOOK

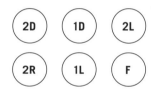

The red button is the first one pressed.

PAGE 40 LONG LAUGH

What did the skeleton take to the mob potluck?

SPARE RIBS

PAGE 41 GETTIN' CRAFTY

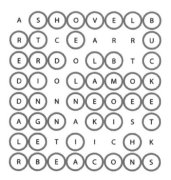

A CARROT ON A STICK

PAGE 42 TRUE OR FALSE?

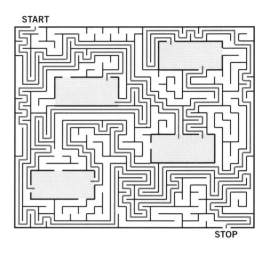

PAGE 43 GO WITH THE FLOW CHART

REDSTONE CIRCUIT

PAGE 44 INSIDE INFO

ON DECEMBER 24-26, CHESTS LOOK LIKE WRAPPED PRESENTS

PAGE 45 CREEPER DESTROYERS

Jack - 1; Sylvie - 2; Veronica - 3; Oscar - 4; Xavier - 5

PAGE 46 WHOOPS!

NET, NAPS, STAR

What did Alex get when she accidentally splashed her mom and dad with a Potion of Invisibility?

TRANSPARENTS

PAGE 47 WHAT'S FOR DINNER?

Emperor Nethero - Potato

Call me Fishmale - Pufferfish

Enderslayer - Carrot

4321Blastoff - Rotten flesh

PAGE 48 SCORE MORE ORE

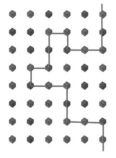

PAGE 49 TRADING JO(S)

Joanne - Librarian

Joni - Priest

Joseph - Butcher

Jorge - Blacksmith

PAGE 50 THE LOCKED DOOR

Liam - red, Ami - green, Lain - yellow, Ali - blue

Lain's yellow wool "key" unlocks the door.

PAGE 51 ZOMBIE FRIENDS

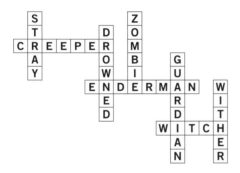

What did the zombie's friends say when he introduced his girlfriend?

GEEZ, WHERE DID YOU DIG HER UP?

PAGE 52 ALEX SAYS: OWN YOUR MINE BUSINESS

FIND DIAMONDS DEEP IN LEVEL TWELVE.

It's the best place to mine for diamonds.

PAGE 53 WHEEL OF FORTUNE #3

ENCHANTED DIAMOND CHESTPLATE

PAGE 54 HIDDEN ARMOR

```
M R H O R S E A R M O H
A O O R M R A S R O H S
H O R S E A R M R O A E
O E S S R O M S R O H O
R H E A E R E S A S M M
S R O M R A E S R O H R
E S A O H A R M A O O A
A E R E R O M E R S M E
R O M M H S S S M A E S
R H O A E R E S R O H R
O O R R O M R A E S R O
R A M H R A E S R O H H
```

PAGE 55 REFLECTIONS IN THE WATER

A LOYALTY ENCHANTMENT BRINGS YOUR THROWN TRIDENT BACK

PAGE 56 SQUARED UP: LOGICAL LOOT

S	B	R	W
R	W	S	B
B	R	W	S
W	S	B	R

PAGE 57 FLOWERS TO DYE FOR

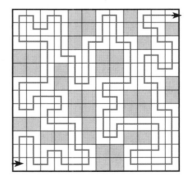

PAGE 58 SHIP SHAPE

UPDATE AQUATIC

CORAL

DOLPHIN

SHIPWRECK

PHANTOM

SEA PICKLES

What happened in the wreck between the red ship and the blue ship?

THE SAILORS WERE MAROONED

PAGE 59 ENCHANTED TRAP DOOR

2D	1L	2D	1L
3R	1R	2L	1D
1R	1U	F	2U

The red button is the first one pressed.

PAGE 60 TALL TALE

Did you hear about the famous skeleton artist?
SHE WAS A SKULL-PTOR

PAGE 61 ANIMALS, ANIMALS EVERYWHERE

BUILD A DIRT ISLAND IN A LAKE TO GROW A STEADY SUPPLY OF WHEAT

PAGE 62 LETTER HUNT

NETHER STAR

PAGE 63 MATH MOBS

6

PAGE 64 SO MUCH FOR PEACEFUL!

LLAMAS CAN CAUSE DAMAGE TO PLAYERS IN PEACEFUL MODE

PAGE 65 BABY'S FAVORITE TOY

What is a baby zombie's favorite toy?
A DEADY BEAR

PAGE 66 HIDDEN HAZARD

29			23	21	11	83	23
41	63	67			65	13	49
35	7	93	47	61			27
25	97	59	31	47	5	15	61
53							3
	89	71	19	79	95	53	
	75	39	1	29	71	95	
5							23
17	45	67	85	35	47	59	35
55			3				57
	13	27		25	65	83	
	11	15	91	51	37	51	
33							81
21	71	85	5	45	93	57	43
				13	43	1	63
69	9	97					77
1	33	31		7	49	29	
73	27	15					85
			55	45	9		21
17	61	91	87	73	37	11	69
	79	37					41
81	55			51	77	99	
89	57	65		41	15	63	
33	7	39	53	17	99	3	31
43							87
	25	67	59	67	19	9	
	49	39	3	19	75	19	

PAGE 67 WHOSE BIOME IS THIS?

Squ88mish - Desert

MineQueen - Deep ocean

ZipDooDa - Jungle

Knowitall - Mountains

PAGE 68 MOB DROPS

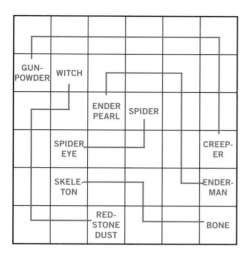

PAGE 69 SURPRISE!

Raya - Chicken

Marcus - Bat

Jess - Flower

Sachin - Creeper

PAGE 71 WHAT ZOMBIES WANT

Why did the zombie attack the skeleton?

IT WANTED HIS BONE AND MARROW

PAGE 72 WHODUNNIT?

PUFFERFISH, MULE, EVOKER

SQUID, PIG, ENDERMAN, HORSE

SHULKER

SPIDER

PAGE 73 WHEEL OF FORTUNE #4

PER BEND SINISTER INVERTED BANNER

Do you know what this banner looks like?

PAGE 74 SEED FINDER

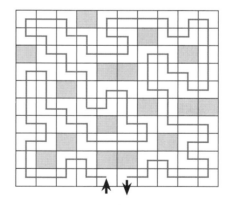

PAGE 75 IN THE BEGINNING . . .

ORIGINALLY, VILLAGE MOBS WERE TO BE PIGMEN

PAGE 77 BOUNTIFUL HARVEST

PAGE 78 NAME SHIFTING

SKELETON

SKELTONE

SKEABONE

SHEABONE

HEADBONE

BONEHEAD

PAGE 79 ENCHANTED BOW AND ARROW

(3D) (2D) (**1L**) (2D)

(1R) (2D) (1R) (2D)

(2U) (1R) (1D) (3L)

(2U) (F) (2U) (3U)

The red button is the first one pressed.

PAGE 80 WHICH WITCH?

What do you call a witch that spawns in the desert?
A SAND WITCH

PAGE 81 PICK A POTION

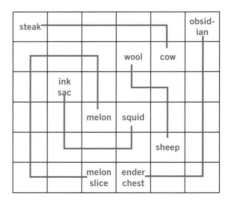

AN INSTANT DAMAGE IV POTION CAN KILL A PLAYER AT ONCE

PAGE 82 TEXT STRINGS

COMMANDS

PAGE 83 ADDITIONAL MATH MOBS

16

PAGE 84 FLOWER POWER

FLOWERS WILL GENERATE IN LAVA, CAVES, AND ABANDONED MINESHAFTS

PAGE 85 A RARE FIND

SPONGE

PAGE 86 MINER HUMOR

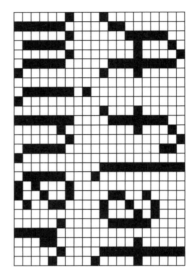

PAGE 87 DROP MATCH

PAGE 88 A COLD RECEPTION

SET, FIB, ROT

What do you get from a hostile wolf in the snowy taiga?

FROSTBITE